EXPLORING WORLD CULTURES

Nicaragua

Alicia Z. Klepeis

Cavendish
Square

New York

Published in 2021 by Cavendish Square Publishing, LLC
243 5th Avenue, Suite 136, New York, NY 10016

Website: cavendishsq.com

This publication represents the opinions and views of the author based on his or her personal experience, knowledge, and research. The information in this book serves as a general guide only. The author and publisher have used their best efforts in preparing this book and disclaim liability rising directly or indirectly from the use and application of this book.

All websites were available and accurate when this book was sent to press.

Library of Congress Cataloging-in-Publication Data

Names: Klepeis, Alicia, 1971- author.
Title: Nicaragua / Alicia Z. Klepeis.
Description: First edition. | New York : Cavendish Square Publishing, 2021. | Series: Exploring world cultures | Includes index.
Identifiers: LCCN 2019050407 (print) | LCCN 2019050408 (ebook) | ISBN 9781502656872 (library binding) | ISBN 9781502656858 (paperback) | ISBN 9781502656865 (set) | ISBN 9781502656889 (ebook) |
Subjects: LCSH: Nicaragua--Juvenile literature.
Classification: LCC F1523.2 .K55 2021 (print) | LCC F1523.2 (ebook) | DDC 972.85--dc23
LC record available at https://lccn.loc.gov/2019050407
LC ebook record available at https://lccn.loc.gov/2019050408

Editor: Kristen Susienka
Copy Editor: Nathan Heidelberger
Designer: Jessica Nevins

The photographs in this book are used by permission and through the courtesy of: Cover WORLDWIDE photo/Alamy Stock Photo; p. 4 Karen Kasmauski/Corbis NX/Getty Images Plus; p. 5 Travel With Passion/Shutterstock.com; p. 6 pavalena/Shutterstock.com; p. 7 Tanguy de Saint-Cyr/Shutterstock.com; p. 8 Milosz Maslanka/Shutterstock.com; p. 9 Mark Reinstein/Corbis via Getty Images; p. 10 Artur_Sarkisyan/Shutterstock.com; pp. 11, 13, 22, 23 INTI OCON/AFP via Getty Images; p. 12 gaborbasch/Shutterstock.com; p. 14 David Havel/Shutterstock.com; p. 15 Beverly Speed/Shutterstock.com; p. 16 Shawn Talbot/Shutterstock.com; p. 17 Dino Fracchia/Alamy Stock Photo; p. 18 © Jonathan Kingston/Cavan Images; p. 19 Riderfoot/Shutterstock.com; p. 20 © iStockphoto.com/JESUSDEFUENSANTA; p. 21 HECTOR RETAMAL/AFP via Getty Images; p. 24 DavorLovincic/iStock Unreleased/Getty Images; p. 25 Marek Poplawski/Shutterstock.com; p. 26 Matyas Rehak/Shutterstock.com; p. 27 Chrispictures/Shutterstock.com; p. 28 Wei Seah/Shutterstock.com; p. 29 rj lerich/Shutterstock.com.

Some of the images in this book illustrate individuals who are models. The depictions do not imply actual situations or events.

CPSIA compliance information: Batch #CS20CSQ: For further information contact Cavendish Square Publishing LLC, New York, New York, at 1-877-980-4450.

Printed in the United States of America

Find us on

Contents

Nicaragua is a special place. People have lived there for thousands of years. Throughout its history, different outside groups have ruled what's now Nicaragua. The Spanish are one

Beekeeping is a special job in Nicaragua. Here, a person is gathering honey.

example. Nicaragua is an independent country today. More than 6 million people live there.

Nicaraguans do many different jobs. Some work in hotels or markets. Others have jobs in schools or restaurants. Factories make items such as clothing and cigars that people smoke. Farmers grow coffee and sugarcane.

There are many beautiful places to visit in Nicaragua. Lovely lakes and islands are located there. Tourists, or visitors, from around the world come to the nation's beaches and

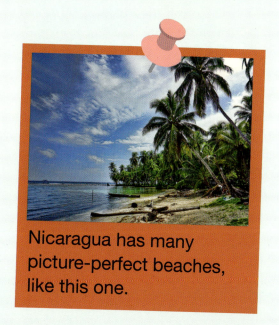

Nicaragua has many picture-perfect beaches, like this one.

villages. Nature parks, or reserves, are home to amazing animals, including monkeys and jaguars.

The **culture** of Nicaragua is rich. People create different kinds of art and music. Nicaraguans also enjoy sports. Celebrations and festivals happen all year long. Nicaragua is a great country to explore!

Geography

Nicaragua is in Central America. Honduras is its neighbor to the north. Costa Rica lies to the south. The Caribbean Sea sits on Nicaragua's east coast. The Pacific Ocean

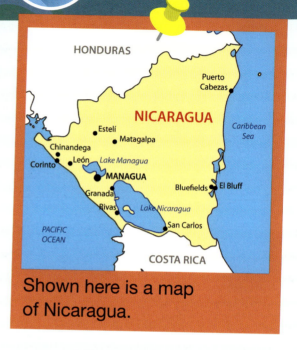

Shown here is a map of Nicaragua.

borders Nicaragua to the west. Nicaragua covers 50,336 square miles (130,370 square kilometers).

Nicaragua has **lowlands** between its Pacific coast and Lake Managua. Most of the country's people live in this area. Volcanoes run through

FACT!

Lake Nicaragua is the largest lake in Central America.

6

Earthquakes and Storms

Nicaragua often experiences earthquakes and **tropical storms.** In 2017, Tropical Storm Nate caused heavy rain and floods.

western Nicaragua, and many mountains are located in the country's center. Plains make up much of the east. The Mosquito (or Miskito)

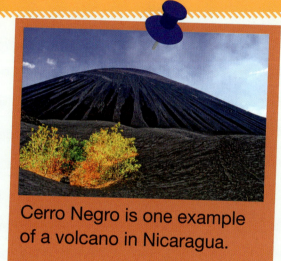

Cerro Negro is one example of a volcano in Nicaragua.

Coast, also to the east, is a swampy area. Most rivers in Nicaragua, like the Coco and the San Juan, flow into the Caribbean Sea.

Nicaragua has a warm, **humid** climate, or weather, but it's cooler in the mountains. May to November is the country's rainy season.

People have lived in what's now Nicaragua for thousands of years. By 1500 BCE, many native tribes lived there. Over time, people started growing beans, corn, and other crops. As early as

El Calvario Church in the city of León was built in the 1700s, when Spain ruled what's now Nicaragua.

300 CE, they were trading with people from other countries, like what's now known as Colombia.

In the early 1500s, Spanish explorers arrived. Spain ruled Nicaragua for 300 years. The country

FACT!

While Spain ruled most of Nicaragua, Great Britain once controlled the Mosquito Coast area.

Violeta Chamorro was the first female president of Nicaragua. She served in this role from 1990 to 1997.

President Violeta Chamorro of Nicaragua is shown here addressing the US Congress in 1991.

declared independence from Spain in 1821. Nicaragua was then part of Mexico. It soon became part of the United Provinces of Central America. This federation, or group, also included Honduras, El Salvador, Guatemala, and Costa Rica. Nicaragua became its own country in 1838.

Since independence, Nicaragua has been through wars and other hard times. Hopefully, the nation will have a brighter future in the years to come.

VOTE ✓

Nicaragua is a **republic**. It has 15 departments, which are like states. The country also has two independent areas on its Caribbean coast. The nation's capital city is Managua.

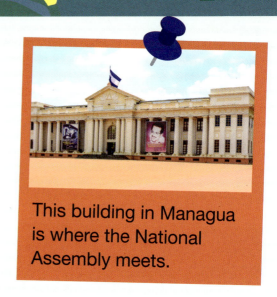

This building in Managua is where the National Assembly meets.

Nicaragua's government has three parts: legislative, judicial, and executive. The legislative part is called the National Assembly. Members of

FACT!

In Nicaragua's past, many leaders were **dictators.** This made it hard for Nicaragua to grow as a country.

Women hold 45 percent of the seats in Nicaragua's National Assembly.

the National Assembly write new laws. Courts make up the judicial part of Nicaragua's government. The courts follow the nation's constitution, which describes all the basic

These women are counting the votes for the 2016 presidential election in Nicaragua. People vote for their leaders in this country.

laws of Nicaragua. It's been used since 1987. The courts also decide if laws are fair.

The executive part is made up of the president and the Council of Ministers. This group helps the president run the government.

The Economy

Nicaragua is Central America's poorest country. However, it trades with countries around the world. Nicaragua's most important trading partners include the United States,

A female police officer works in her office in the city of Estelí. Women make up about 30 percent of Nicaragua's police force.

China, Costa Rica, and El Salvador. The country's money is the Nicaraguan córdoba.

Over half of the workers in Nicaragua work in jobs that help people. This includes police officers, tour guides, and teachers. Some work

FACT!

Beef, shrimp, and lobster are popular foods **exported** from Nicaragua.

Earning Money Abroad

Many people move away from Nicaragua and send money back to their families. The money they send home helps the country grow.

on construction sites or in national parks. However, many people have trouble finding work or earning enough money.

This worker cleans coffee plants on a farm. More than 300,000 Nicaraguans work in jobs connected to coffee.

Factory workers in Nicaragua make products like knit sweaters and T-shirts. Nicaraguan factories also produce different kinds of wire.

Gold is an important export. It comes from the country's mines. Nicaraguan farmers grow crops like coffee, rice, sugarcane, and peanuts.

Many kinds of plants and animals live in Nicaragua. Trees that grow here include mahogany and quebracho (also known as axbreaker). Orchids and ferns are other forest plants in this country.

The violet sabrewing is a large hummingbird that lives in Nicaragua's forests, among other locations.

The Bosawás Biosphere Reserve is in Nicaragua. Animals and plants are kept safe on its land. Jaguars, pumas, and scarlet macaws live there. Fish, turtles, and sharks live in the Caribbean Sea.

FACT!

The Baird's tapir and the harpy eagle are two **endangered** animals found in Nicaragua.

Energy from Volcanoes

Almost half of Nicaragua's electricity comes from **renewable energy sources** such as waterpower. There's a huge wind farm near Lake Nicaragua. The country even uses molten, or melted, rock beneath volcanoes to help make electricity!

Major problems in Nicaragua include pollution and the loss of forests. Much of the water and air in the country is dirty. Forests have been cut down for

A squirrel fish swims in the waters off Nicaragua's Caribbean coast.

years to make room for farms and cattle ranches. Many animals lose their homes when this happens.

Nicaraguan locals often refer to themselves as Nicas. However, outsiders usually call them Nicaraguans.

Nicaraguan children often go to schools like the one shown here.

About 70 percent of Nicaraguans are mestizo. This means they have both European and Native American relatives. White people are the second-largest group in Nicaragua. They make up about 17 percent of the country's population.

About 9 percent of Nicaraguans are black.

The average person in Nicaragua can expect to live 74 years.

The Rama

The Rama are a small native group in Nicaragua. They live on the Caribbean coast, often in wooden houses built on tall poles called stilts. Many Rama men work as fishermen.

Two Rama women are shown here in their village on Rama Key, an island on the Caribbean coast.

Most are **descendants** of slaves brought to the country centuries ago. They often live on the country's Caribbean coast. Many of the Native Americans in Nicaragua live there as well. The Miskito and Mayanga peoples are two examples. Unfortunately, both the black and native peoples living in Nicaragua are often treated poorly.

17

In Nicaragua, about 60 percent of people live in cities and towns. The nation's largest city is Managua. Crime is a big problem in cities.

These homes on the Mosquito Coast are built on stilts to prevent flooding during the rainy season.

In the countryside, many people work on farms. Roads are often made of dirt or rock, making travel hard.

Many Nicaraguan children go to school for at least six years. Some go on to high school, called secondary school. There are also universities in big

FACT!

More than 1 million people live in the capital city of Managua.

Working Women

More than half of Nicaraguan small businesses are owned by women. Some women run food stands at markets. Others create businesses that sell medicine for pets, cleaning supplies, or other goods.

A woman sells roasted corn on the cob at a market in the city of Managua.

cities for people to go to after secondary school. Schools where people learn a skill like carpentry are available too.

Throughout Nicaragua, many people struggle to have enough to eat. Not all homes have running water. Men and women sometimes take jobs far away from their families to earn money. Children may leave school to help their families.

Religion plays an important part in the lives of many Nicaraguans. Most people are Christian. Half of the nation's population is Roman Catholic. Roughly one-third of Nicaraguans are Protestant.

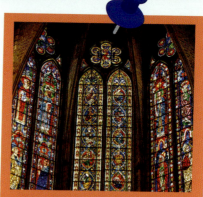

Stained-glass windows are just one beautiful feature in the León Cathedral.

Like Christians all over the world, Nicaraguans celebrate Christmas and Easter. The country also has some special religious celebrations. An event called La Gritería happens on December 7. Families put figures of Mary,

FACT!

The León Cathedral in Nicaragua is the largest church in Central America.

Foods for Lent

Lent is a Catholic time of prayer and giving things up. Catholics don't eat beef, chicken, or other meats on Fridays during Lent. Instead, Nicaraguans eat foods like iguana or seafood.

Jesus's mother, in front of their homes. In the evening, groups travel the area, singing songs about Mary. People give candy, little toys, or other items to the singers. Fireworks are set off at night.

A Catholic child in Managua sings as part of the festivities during La Gritería.

There's no official religion in Nicaragua. People have the freedom to believe what they want. A small amount of Nicaraguans practice religions other than Christianity.

Language

Most people in Nicaragua speak Spanish. Today, Spanish is the country's official language. Other languages spoken include Sumo, Miskito, Creole English, and Rama. Some of these languages, like

A man holds up a sign, written in Spanish, during a peaceful **demonstration** in Managua in April 2018.

Rama and Sumo, are native languages.

The government of Nicaragua uses Spanish. Businesspeople use Spanish too. Some people in

FACT!

More than 130,000 people in Nicaragua speak the native Miskito language.

A New Language

People who are hard of hearing can use Nicaraguan Sign Language (NSL). It was started in the 1970s and 1980s. The number of users of NSL is growing.

This woman is teaching a sign language class in Nicaragua.

Nicaragua's cities speak English. In addition to English and Spanish, Garífuna and Creole are popular languages among the country's black population.

Children in Nicaraguan schools have their classes in Spanish. Secondary schools typically offer English classes too.

23

Arts and Festivals

All over Nicaragua, people enjoy art. Some Nicaraguan artists create paintings. Others make amazing art on the sides of buildings. People in the city of Masaya often make colorful hammocks. The

This craft market in Masaya offers the hammocks, woodwork, and clothing Nicaragua is known for.

village of Catarina is known for making beautiful wooden objects and bamboo baskets.

Music is an important part of Nicaraguan culture. Salsa is a popular type of dance music.

Majo y Mafe is a popular female rap group in Nicaragua.

The city of Granada has hosted a poetry festival since 2005. Poets from around the world celebrate by reading poems in places around the city. In 2019, it was canceled because of problems with the government.

The coastal town of Bluefields is known for reggae music, or music from the Caribbean. The marimba is Nicaragua's national instrument. Its

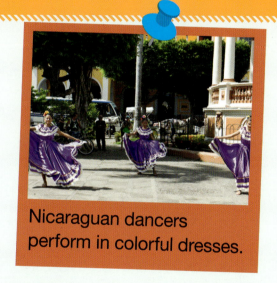

Nicaraguan dancers perform in colorful dresses.

wooden pieces are hit with sticks.

Independence Day in Nicaragua is on September 15. This holiday marks when the nation gained independence from Spain.

Fun and Play

There are lots of ways to have fun in Nicaragua. Many people enjoy sports. Baseball is the country's most popular sport. Baseball diamonds, or fields, are found in towns and villages across the nation. People in Nicaragua also like playing soccer, basketball, and volleyball.

A local baseball game takes place in the town of Somoto, located in northern Nicaragua.

Nicaraguans old and young like to dance. It's common for local schools to host dances on weekends. Kids and teenagers also enjoy time

FACT!

Visitors to Masaya National Park can peek into a steaming volcano.

Erasmo Ramírez

Erasmo Ramírez is a professional baseball player from Nicaragua. He has played for US teams including the Seattle Mariners and Tampa Bay Rays.

with friends in parks. Going to the beach is a popular activity. Biking is too.

Visitors to Nicaragua like to tour nature reserves and beaches. They also like

A group of boys poses for a picture during a soccer game in Nicaragua.

to climb volcanoes, camp, and visit the country's old churches and buildings.

Chess is a common game to play in Nicaragua. Children also enjoy playing *chibolas*, or marbles.

Food

Rice and beans are part of most meals in Nicaragua. *Gallo pinto* is the country's national dish. It's made of fried rice, red or black beans, and spices. Corn is another main part of

Gallo pinto is served here alongside a salad and a tortilla.

the Nicaraguan diet. It's used to make tortillas. *Nacatamal* is a popular corn dish. *Chicha* is a drink made from corn, sugar, and water.

FACT!

Unusual ice cream flavors in Nicaragua include lavender-blueberry and cheesecake guava.

Tres Leches Cake

Tres leches (three milks) cake is a popular dessert in Nicaragua. This cake is soaked in different kinds of milk. It's very sweet and tasty!

Many tropical fruits grow in Nicaragua. People here often enjoy mangoes, papayas, bananas, and passion fruit.

On Nicaragua's Big Corn Island, fish is served with salad and *tostones*, or fried plantains.

Nicaragua's Caribbean coast has its own special foods. *Róndon* is a dish that includes turtle meat, fish, and pork or red meat. It also contains herbs and peppers. *Gaubul* is a drink made of sugar, coconut water, milk, and cooked plantain (a type of banana).

Glossary

culture   The beliefs and way of life of a group of people.

demonstration   A public display of feelings or support.

descendant   Someone related to an individual person or a group of people who lived at an earlier time.

dictator   A person who rules with total authority, often in a cruel manner.

endangered   Describing a plant or animal that might go extinct, or die out.

export   To sell goods to another country.

humid   Describing heavy air that makes the temperature feel warmer than it is.

lowland   An area of a country that is usually flat and has no high mountains.

religion   A set of beliefs about a god or gods.

renewable energy source   A type of power that can be used over and over again without running out, like wind, solar, or waterpower.

republic   A type of government in which people can choose their leaders.

tropical storm   A strong, rotating storm with winds over 39 miles (63 kilometers) per hour; stronger tropical storms are called hurricanes.

Find Out More

Books

Engle, Margarita. *With a Star in My Hand: Rubén Darío, Poetry Hero*. New York, NY: Atheneum Books for Young Readers, 2020.

Owings, Lisa. *Nicaragua*. Minneapolis, MN: Bellwether Media, 2015.

Website

National Geographic Kids: Nicaragua

https://kids.nationalgeographic.com/explore/countries/nicaragua

Find out all about Nicaragua from *National Geographic*'s kid-friendly website.

Video

Lonely Planet: Introducing Nicaragua

https://www.youtube.com/watch?v=M6ZLfGZv5_Q

This video shows cities, beautiful beaches, and other popular activities and places in Nicaragua.

Index

About the Author

Alicia Z. Klepeis began her career at the National Geographic Society. She is the author of over 100 kids' books, including *Moon Base and Beyond: The Lunar Gateway to Deep Space*, *The World's Strangest Foods*, and *Francisco's Kites*. She would love to hike in Nicaragua's forests and explore the country's beaches and volcanoes.